NEVER FORGET

A NAME OR FACE

DOMINIC O'BRIEN

NEVER FORGET

A NAME OR FACE

CHRONICLE BOOKS
SAN FRANCISCO

To anyone battling against
memory-related difficulties.

Never Forget A Name or Face
Dominic O'Brien

First published in the United States
in 2002 by Chronicle Books LLC.

Copyright © 2002 by Duncan Baird
Publishers
Text Copyright © 2002 by Duncan
Baird Publishers
Commissioned Artwork Copyright
© 2002 by Duncan Baird Publishers

Conceived, Created, and Designed by
Duncan Baird Publishers Ltd
Sixth Floor, Castle House
75–76 Wells Street, London W1T 3QH

Library of Congress Cataloging-In-
Publication Data available.

ISBN: 0-8118-3634-7

Typeset in Helvetica Condensed
Cover Design by Jessica Grunwald
Manufactured in Thailand

Distributed in Canada by
Raincoast Books
9050 Shaughnessy Street
Vancouver, B.C. V6P 6E5

10 9 8 7 6 5 4 3 2 1

Chronicle Books LLC
85 Second Street
San Francisco, CA 94105
www.chroniclebooks.com

CONTENTS

INTRODUCTION

How many times have you been introduced to somebody, only to find that a minute or so later their name has been mysteriously erased from your memory? Embarrassing, isn't it?

I, too, used to have a problem remembering names for any length of time. And yet now I regularly give presentations where I am introduced to 80,

90 or 100 or more people just once, after which I am able to reel off, not only their first names, but also their surnames. "How *do* you do it?" they ask.

In this book, I reveal exactly how I do it, sharing with you the techiques that will help you to never again forget a person's name and face. The methods are tried and tested – they were ❯

designed for competition and they have helped me become the World Memory Champion eight times.

But don't worry, you don't have to be a memory champion to master memorizing names and faces. After a little practice, you'll probably wonder why you used to find it so difficult.

I hope you enjoy learning the techniques in this book – be sure to practise them on friends and colleagues, socially or in the workplace. Before you know it, they'll be asking you: "How *do* you do it?"

Dominic O'Brien

SYMBOLS USED IN THIS BOOK

? MEMORY TECHNIQUE

! MEMORY WISDOM

✓ MEMORY IN ACTION

WHY DO WE HAVE SUCH DIFFICULTY REMEMBERING NAMES AND FACES?

The number-one complaint that people make to me about their memories is their inability to match names to faces. Actually, we are very good at remembering faces – it is recalling the names that go with them that gives us trouble. This is because, as our >

species evolved we needed to be able to recognize immediately who were our friends and who were our enemies, to ensure that we didn't run into any trouble.

The ability to remember a name, on the other hand, is a skill that we have needed to acquire only recently, and our brains have not yet developed a particular mechanism that can match names to faces automatically.

LET ME PROVE TO YOU HOW INSTINCTIVELY GOOD YOU ARE
AT REMEMBERING FACES. ON THESE TWO PAGES YOU WILL
FIND 9 FACES. LOOK AT EACH ONE
BRIEFLY, AND THEN TURN OVER TO
THE NEXT PAGE. >

HERE ARE 10 FACES. YOU HAVE SEEN 9 OF THEM ALREADY. LOOK AT THEM CAREFULLY AND TRY TO SPOT THE "NEW" FACE. >

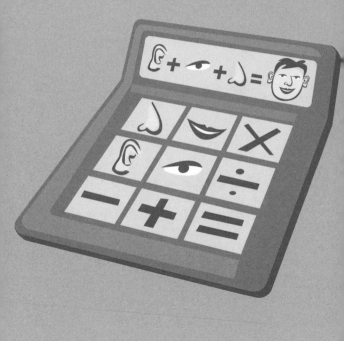

Easy, wasn't it? Research shows that we are better at remembering images when we make associations with them. In 1974 scientists found that when volunteers were asked not only to look at faces but also to assess the qualities they thought the faces showed (for example, kindness, honesty and so on) the volunteers' ability to remember those faces was enhanced.

WHAT'S IN A NAME?

Let's now look at names. Whereas in the past people had names associated with their character or trade – for example, Fred Fullalove or Bob (the) Baker – which were easy to remember, today we often find ourselves having to remember more challenging names, from all over the world, that suggest no obvious link with the person. ❯

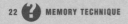

In other words, our names no longer describe, say, our personality or our profession. This means we need to create an artificial link between a person and their name. How? Well, to create

an *association* we need to use our *imagination*. And to make the association stick we need a *location*. *Association, imagination* and *location* are my three keys to a better memory.

TIME TO REMEMBER

Our ability to remember is influenced by many factors, such as how tired we are, whether we have just eaten, even what time of day it is. Research has shown that, for most of us, the best time to perform memory tasks is during mid- to late morning, and the worst time is for about an hour immediately after lunch.

"PLACING" PEOPLE

Imagine you are out walking when you see someone vaguely familiar coming toward you. You wrack your brains to remember their name, but no matter how hard you try, you just cannot "place" them. The key to solving the problem is the word "place", because once you can recall the location where you met, the name will come back to you in a flash.

NAMES AND PLACES

I realized I could exploit our instinct to link a person with a place by associating each new person I met with a location that reminded me of their name. I call this method "Names and Places". For example, if I am introduced to someone called Tony, I might imagine him standing outside Prime Minister Tony Blair's residence at 10 Downing Street. ❯

In this way I am taking the Tony I've just met out of his surroundings and transporting him to a place that will trigger his name. Of course, the place needn't be a famous one. Say I meet someone called Peggy – the first thing her name conjures up is a line of clothes pegs, hanging on the washing line in my garden. So I envisage Peggy there, "pegging" out washing. ❯

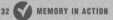

Now I would like you to try your hand at "Names and Places". Link each of the following five names with a location that helps you to remember that name: Don, Gemma, Sidney, Carol and James.

How did you get on? You could, for example, have linked Don to a tennis court at Wimble*don*; *Gemma*, to a jewelry

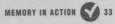

STORE; SIDNEY, TO THE OPERA HOUSE IN THE
AUSTRALIAN CITY OF SYDNEY; CAROL, TO THE LOCAL
CHURCH WHICH HOLDS A CAROL SERVICE EVERY
CHRISTMAS; AND JAMES TO YOUR GYM (JIM). >

Returning to Tony, let's extend the link to include his surname, which is Ransome. This name makes me think of ransom money, and so I visualize Tony outside 10 Downing Street as before, but now clutching a bag of money. Whereas before we simply linked the first name with a place, we extend the association by linking the person also with an object (or action) representing the surname. >

LET'S NOW TAKE THE OTHER EXAMPLE INVOLVING PEGGY. HER SURNAME IS HARPER, SO I NOW THINK IMMEDIATELY OF PEGGY PEGGING OUT HARPS ON THE CLOTHES LINE.

NOW IT'S YOUR TURN TO LINK IN SOME SURNAMES. BELOW I'VE ADDED SURNAMES TO THE LIST OF FIVE FORENAMES YOU PREVIOUSLY LINKED TO LOCATIONS (SEE PP.32–3). THEY ARE: DON WEATHERBY, GEMMA RUSSELL, SIDNEY SANDERS, CAROL RAILTON AND JAMES WIGMORE.

HOW DID YOU GET ON? HERE'S A COUPLE OF EXAMPLES. YOU COULD LINK DON'S SURNAME WEATHERBY TO THE TENNIS COURT AT WIMBLEDON BY IMAGINING RAIN STOPPING PLAY (BAD *WEATHER*); OR YOU COULD LINK IN GEMMA'S SURNAME, RUSSELL, BY THINKING OF HER WRAPPING UP JEWELRY IN TISSUE PAPER THAT *RUSTLES*; AND SO ON.

Cecile
Cecile

Jerry
Jerry

Lara

Lara

Zoë Zo

Marvin, Marvin

Barbara
Barbara

Wayne Wayne

James... Jam

Antonio
Antonio

Maria Ma

REPEAT THE NAME

Once you have been introduced to someone, try to use their name once or twice in your conversation together. By repeating their name you are helping to consolidate it in your memory. And the person you have just met will feel flattered that you find them interesting enough to remember their name.

LOOKS FAMILIAR

In this method, you link the person who's name you wish to memorize with someone familiar. They could be a famous person, say a movie star or a singer, or they could be a relative or a friend. The resemblance can be slight or strong. The important thing is that your brain associates your new acquaintance with the familiar person. ❯

HERE'S HOW IT WORKS. LET'S SAY YOU'VE JUST MET
TED, WHO REMINDS YOU OF THE GOLFER, TIGER WOODS.
YOUR BRAIN IMMEDIATELY LINKS TED WITH TIGER. NEXT,
YOU NEED TO LOCATE TED MENTALLY IN A PLACE THAT YOU

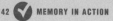

WOULD NORMALLY ASSOCIATE WITH TIGER WOODS —
WHERE ELSE, BUT ON A GOLF COURSE! YOU NOW HAVE
A LOCATION IN WHICH TO PUT HIM. FINALLY, YOU NEED
TO LINK TED'S NAME TO THE GOLF COURSE BY THINKING
UP A SUITABLE IMAGE. HOW ABOUT A *TED*DY BEAR? >

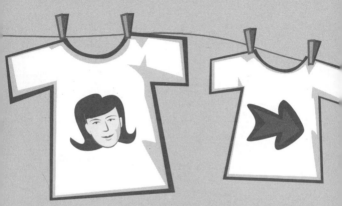

SO THE WAY TO REMEMBER TED IS TO FORM AN *ASSOCIATION* WITH SOMEONE FAMILIAR (TIGER WOODS), ANCHOR HIM TO A *LOCATION* LINKED WITH TIGER (A GOLF COURSE), AND USE YOUR *IMAGINATION* TO DEPICT TED IN A WAY THAT CONJURES UP HIS NAME (AS A TEDDY BEAR).

TRY THIS TECHNIQUE TO REMEMBER THE NAMES OF THE NEXT FIVE PEOPLE YOU MEET. >

LET'S NOW APPLY THE SAME PRINCIPLE TO TED'S SURNAME.
WE HAVE ALREADY ANCHORED HIM TO A LOCATION (THE GOLF
COURSE) AND DEPICTED HIM IN A WAY THAT
CONJURES UP HIS NAME (AS A

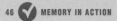

TEDDY BEAR). NOW WE ARE GOING TO INTRODUCE HIS SURNAME, WHICH IS FORD. SO WE IMAGINE THE TEDDY BEAR ON THE GOLF COURSE AS BEFORE, BUT THIS TIME WE ENVISAGE HIM SITTING IN A FORD CAR. IN THIS WAY WE HAVE INCLUDED THE SURNAME SIMPLY BY ADDING IN AN EXTRA ASSOCIATION — IN THIS CASE, THE CAR. >

LET'S LOOK AT ANOTHER EXAMPLE. THIS TIME YOU ARE INTRODUCED TO A NEW BUSINESS ACQUAINTANCE CALLED ELLA POOLE, WHO REMINDS YOU OF THE MOVIE STAR MERYL STREEP. YOU START OFF BY IMAGINING ELLA IN A PLACE THAT YOU ASSOCIATE WITH MERYL STREEP – A FILM SET.

THEN YOU NEED AN IMAGE TO ANCHOR THE NAME TO THE LOCATION. THE NAME "ELLA" SOUNDS LIKE THE PREFIX OF "*ELE*PHANT", AND SO YOU VISUALIZE AN ELEPHANT CHARGING AROUND

THE FILM SET, GENERALLY CAUSING HAVOC BY KNOCKING OVER LIGHTS AND CAMERAS, AND SO ON.

NOW YOU ARE GOING TO INTRODUCE ELLA'S SURNAME, WHICH IS POOLE. SO YOU IMAGINE THE ELEPHANT ON THE FILM SET AS BEFORE, AND THEN YOU ENVISAGE IT PLUNGING INTO A NEARBY SWIMMING POOL. SO AGAIN YOU HAVE INCLUDED THE SURNAME BY INCLUDING AN EXTRA LINK — THE SWIMMING POOL.

FIRST IS BEST

When making associations, always stick with the first image that comes into your mind (no matter how absurd this mental picture may seem to you on later reflection). Your brain's initial reaction is intuitive – the image that first comes to mind is the one that you are most likely to recall automatically.

MEMORY MUSIC

Recent research suggests that listening to classical music, especially Mozart, can aid memory recall. Try it yourself. Put on some Mozart or other classical music and memorize twelve faces from photos, with the people's names. Repeat with another set of photos, but this time in silence. Then compare your results.

WHAT'S MY LINE?

What if you meet someone who just doesn't resemble anyone familiar? Then you try "What's My Line" – a technique that involves using your imagination to guess what the person might do for a living. Don't try to be accurate – be instinctive. Look at the face and decide that they are, say, an artist or a bank manager, or anything else that comes to mind.

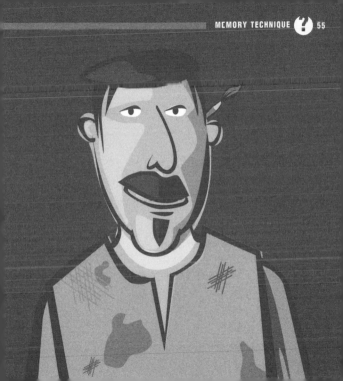

LET'S ASSUME THAT YOU MEET CELIA, WHO YOU THINK LOOKS LIKE A LAWYER. THE NEXT STEP IS TO PUT HER IN A SUITABLE SETTING, AND THE FIRST PLACE THAT SPRINGS TO MIND IS A COURTROOM.

NEXT, YOU NEED TO BRING YOUR IMAGINATION INTO PLAY AGAIN TO LINK HER NAME TO THE LOCATION, SO YOU IMAGINE CELIA HOLDING A DOCUMENT THAT HAS AN OFFICIAL-LOOKING SEAL (A WORD THAT SOUNDS LIKE PART OF THE NAME "CELIA") AT THE BOTTOM.

ONCE THIS ASSOCIATION IS STORED IN YOUR MIND, EVERY TIME YOU MEET CELIA THE IMAGE WILL BE TRIGGERED, AND YOU WILL AUTOMATICALLY RECALL HER NAME.

NOW YOU NEED TO LINK IN HER SURNAME, WHICH IS HEATHCOTE. THIS NAME MAKES ME THINK OF A WARM, PADDED *COAT* (WHICH PRODUCES *HEAT*) AND SO THE FIRST ASSOCIATION THAT SPRINGS TO MY MIND IS CELIA, STILL IN THE COURTROOM HOLDING HER DOCUMENT WITH >

THE SEAL, BUT NOW WRAPPED UP IN HER WARM, PADDED
COAT. NOTICE THAT THIS TIME THE SURNAME IS LINKED
WITH AN ACTION RATHER THAN AN OBJECT. NOW THINK
UP YOUR OWN ASSOCIATION FOR "HEATHCOTE".

LET'S TRY ANOTHER EXAMPLE. SAY YOU MEET A GUY CALLED RODNEY BLACK WHO HAS A WAY OF TALKING THAT REMINDS YOU OF A DOCTOR'S BEDSIDE MANNER. YOUR BRAIN IMMEDIATELY TAKES ADVANTAGE OF THIS THOUGHT >

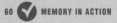

AND CONJURES UP A MENTAL PICTURE OF RODNEY AS A DOCTOR IN A HOSPITAL. THE NEXT STEP IS TO FIND A WAY OF LINKING HIS NAME WITH THE HOSPITAL.

THE FIRST THING THAT COMES INTO YOUR HEAD IS AN IMAGE OF RODNEY EXAMINING CLOSELY AN X-RAY OF A PATIENT'S KNEE THAT HAS A METAL ROD FITTED IN IT (THIS LINKS "ROD" AND "KNEE"). THE FINAL STEP IS TO LINK IN HIS SURNAME – BLACK – BY VISUALIZING HIM WEARING A BLACK MEDICS' COAT,

INSTEAD OF THE USUAL WHITE ONE
HABITUALLY WORN BY DOCTORS.

IF YOU ARE THINKING
THAT IT MAY BE EASY
FOR ME TO MAKE SUCH
IMMEDIATE ASSOCIATIONS,
BUT YOU YOURSELF WILL
NEVER MANAGE IT — BANISH
THOSE THOUGHTS NOW!
REMEMBER, YOUR BRAIN
ALREADY MAKES SIMILAR
ASSOCIATIONS AUTOMATICALLY
AND IN SECONDS. THE ONLY DIFFERENCE HERE IS THAT
YOU ARE CONSCIOUSLY CREATING LINKS. WITH PRACTICE
IT WILL BECOME SECOND NATURE.

MEMORY FOODS

It is vital to eat a healthy diet if we wish to keep our memory in full working order. Foods rich in vitamins A, C and E, such as oranges and red peppers, have been shown to aid memory recall. Oily fish, such as salmon, are another rich source of nutrients good for the brain. Try to eat oily fish at least twice a week.

DIFFICULT NAMES

So far we've looked at making associations with straightforward names, but what if you are introduced to someone who has a long name or a name

that is difficult to pronounce? Well, the same principles apply. All you have to do is simply break the name up into syllables or manageable parts. ❯

TAKE A NAME SUCH AS ROISIN (PRONOUNCED "ROSH-EEN"). LET'S ASSUME THAT YOUR NEW FEMALE ACQUAINTANCE LOOKS LIKE A POLICE OFFICER. HER NAME IS ROISIN BOYLE, AND SO YOU IMAGINE HER *RUSHING* TO CATCH A CRIMINAL. THEN, TO INCLUDE THE SURNAME BOYLE, YOU COULD VISUALIZE ROISIN CARRYING HER BREAKFAST — A *BOILED* EGG.

WHAT IF THE PERSON TO WHOM YOU WERE JUST INTRODUCED WAS CALLED CIARAN (PRONOUNCED "KEY-RAN") O'GRADY? YOUR FIRST IMPRESSION OF HIM IS THAT HE LOOKS LIKE A CHEF. YOU START WITH A MENTAL IMAGE OF CIARAN TURNING THE *KEY* TO UNLOCK THE KITCHEN DOOR AT THE RESTAURANT WHERE HE WORKS. THEN, TO INCLUDE HIS SURNAME, YOU VISUALIZE HIM MAKING GRAVY (WHICH SOUNDS SIMILAR TO "GRADY").

LET'S LOOK AT SOME MORE EXAMPLES. YOU MEET SOMEONE WHO YOU THINK LOOKS LIKE A TEACHER. SHE TURNS OUT TO BE CALLED CARMELITA ROSADO. FIRST YOU IMAGINE HER IN A SCHOOL CAFETERIA, HAVING LUNCH WITH HER PUPILS. THEN, BECAUSE "CARMELITA" SOUNDS LIKE "CARAMEL-EATER", YOU VISUALIZE HER EATING A CARAMEL DESSERT. AND TO BRING IN HER SURNAME ROSADO, YOU ENVISAGE HER SITTING AT A TABLE THAT HAS A CLOTH EMBROIDERED WITH ROSES.

OR, SAY YOU ARE INTRODUCED TO A MAN CALLED ZENON RIVERA, WHO LOOKS LIKE A MUSICIAN. ZENON SOUNDS LIKE "ZEN NUN", SO YOU PICTURE HIM IN YOUR MIND'S EYE PLAYING A TRUMPET, DRESSED IN THE ROBES OF A ZEN BUDDHIST NUN. THEN, TO INCORPORATE HIS SURNAME, YOU SET THE WHOLE SCENE ON A *RIVER*BANK. ›

LET'S JUST TAKE A MOMENT TO REMIND OURSELVES THAT THE KEY TO MEMORIZING DIFFICULT NAMES LIES IN BREAKING THE NAME DOWN INTO SYLLABLES OR SMALLER PARTS.

YOU HAVE JUST BEEN INTRODUCED TO SOMEONE CALLED OLEG KAMINSKY (PRONOUNCED KAM-IN-SKEE), AND YOU

THINK HE LOOKS LIKE A BANKER. THE FIRST IMAGE YOU CONJURE UP IS OF OLEG SITTING AWKWARDLY AT HIS DESK IN THE BANK, COUNTING BANKNOTES. HE IS SITTING AWKWARDLY BECAUSE HE HAS HAD AN ACCIDENT AND HAS ONE *LEG* IN A CAST. YOU THEN IMAGINE HIM CALLING OUT *"COME IN"*, AS A NEW PAIR OF *SKIS* ARE DELIVERED TO HIS OFFICE!

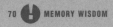

GINGKO BILOBA

Can dietary supplements improve your memory? Research has suggested that taking extract of gingko biloba, either in tablet or liquid form, or as tea, can help memory function by increasing the blood flow to the brain. I always take gingko biloba as part of my preparations before a memory competition.

THE FEATURE LINK

Sometimes when we meet people, we are struck by one particular physical feature, such as their piercing blue eyes, sticking-out ears or long nose. Or we can't help but notice something they wear – unusual glasses, a multi-coloured sweater or rings on every finger. I use this type of memorable characteristic in my technique the "Feature Link". >

LET ME EXPLAIN HOW IT WORKS. SAY YOU MEET A WOMAN CALLED ANGELA MARSHALL. THE THING YOU NOTICE IMMEDIATELY ABOUT HER IS THAT SHE IS WEARING A STRIKING PAIR OF GLASSES — THEY ARE WING-SHAPED. SO, TO CREATE AN ASSOCIATION BETWEEN HER NAME AND HER FACE, YOU IMAGINE A LITTLE ANGEL (ANGELA) ON ONE "WING" OF THE GLASSES. TO INCORPORATE HER SURNAME YOU THEN MENTALLY PLACE A MARSHALL'S BADGE ON THE OTHER "WING" OF THE GLASSES. THEN, EVERY TIME YOU THINK OF THIS IMAGE OF ANGELA, HER NAME WILL AUTOMATICALLY SPRING TO MIND.

HERE ARE SOME MORE EXAMPLES. LET'S ASSUME THAT YOU ARE INTRODUCED TO A GUY CALLED MARCUS, WHO HAS PROMINENT EYEBROWS. TO LINK HIS FIRST NAME WITH HIS FACE YOU IMAGINE MARCUS STANDING IN FRONT

OF A MIRROR, "MARKING" ON HIS EYEBROWS WITH A MAKEUP PENCIL. NOW YOU NEED TO WORK IN HIS SURNAME, WHICH IS BISHOP. THE FIRST THING THAT SPRINGS TO MIND IS A MENTAL PICTURE OF MARCUS WEARING A BISHOP'S MITRE AND ROBES, SO YOU NOW IMAGINE HIM IN THIS OUTFIT, MARKING ON HIS EYEBROWS.

ALTERNATIVELY, LET'S SAY THAT YOU ARE INTRODUCED TO A BUSINESSWOMAN CALLED PENNY WINTERS, WHO HAPPENS TO BE WEARING LEATHER TROUSERS. TO LINK HER FIRST NAME WITH HER FACE, YOU IMAGINE HER SITTING ON YOUR SOFA, WEARING LEATHER TROUSERS, USING A GIANT PEN TO DRAW FLOWERS ON THE KNEES (PEN–KNEE). NOW YOU NEED TO LINK IN HER SURNAME — WINTERS — AND YOU DO THIS SIMPLY BY VISUALIZING SNOW FALLING ALL AROUND HER.

EVOCATIVE SCENTS

By burning scented candles or using certain aromatherapy oils we can increase our powers of recall. Try this bathtime memory enhancer. Sprinkle a few drops of lemon, basil or sandalwood essential oil into your bathwater. Breathe slowly and relax. Then, close your eyes and revisit your most pleasant memories.

HERE AND NOW

Another useful technique that I often use is "Here and Now", which works by associating someone whose name you wish to remember with someone you already know of the same name. You mentally import the person you already know into your present surroundings to help establish a name-link with your new acquaintance. ❯

CONFUSED? WELL, DON'T WORRY. LET'S HAVE A LOOK AT THESE EXAMPLES AND SEE HOW THE TECHNIQUE WORKS. PICTURE YOURSELF AT A PARTY. YOU ARE INTRODUCED TO A WOMAN NAMED MARIA, WHO IS DRINKING AN EXOTIC BLUE COCKTAIL AS SHE CHATS WITH THE HOSTESS.

TO MEMORIZE HER NAME YOU FIRST CONSIDER WHETHER YOU KNOW ANYONE ELSE WITH THE SAME NAME. YOU SUDDENLY RECALL A WORK COLLEAGUE, WHO IS ALSO CALLED MARIA. WONDERFUL! YOU THEN CONJURE UP A MENTAL IMAGE OF YOUR COLLEAGUE MARIA

AND PLACE HER THERE AT THE PARTY, HOLDING A SIMILAR DRINK AND CHATTING WITH THE HOSTESS. ONCE YOUR BRAIN HAS MADE THE ASSOCIATION >

BETWEEN THE TWO MARIAS, YOU WILL BE ABLE TO RECALL
YOUR NEW ACQUAINTANCE'S NAME WHENEVER YOU NEED TO
REMEMBER IT.

YOU NOW NEED TO MEMORIZE YOUR NEW ACQUAINTANCE'S
SURNAME, WHICH IS WALLACE. TO DO THIS YOU MUST
THINK UP A WAY OF LINKING THIS NAME VIVIDLY TO THE
PARTY. IF YOU BREAK THE SURNAME DOWN YOU HAVE
TWO WORDS: "WALL" AND "LACE". SO WHY NOT USE
THEM AS THE BASIS FOR YOUR ASSOCIATION? YOU COULD
THEN IMAGINE YOUR COLLEAGUE MARIA, STILL AT THE
PARTY, BUT NOW SITTING ON A WALL MADE OF LACE.
THIS IMAGE IS ALL THE MORE MEMORABLE BECAUSE
IT IS SO SURREAL.

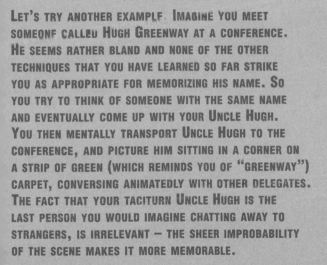

LET'S TRY ANOTHER EXAMPLE. IMAGINE YOU MEET
SOMEONE CALLED HUGH GREENWAY AT A CONFERENCE.
HE SEEMS RATHER BLAND AND NONE OF THE OTHER
TECHNIQUES THAT YOU HAVE LEARNED SO FAR STRIKE
YOU AS APPROPRIATE FOR MEMORIZING HIS NAME. SO
YOU TRY TO THINK OF SOMEONE WITH THE SAME NAME
AND EVENTUALLY COME UP WITH YOUR UNCLE HUGH.
YOU THEN MENTALLY TRANSPORT UNCLE HUGH TO THE
CONFERENCE, AND PICTURE HIM SITTING IN A CORNER ON
A STRIP OF GREEN (WHICH REMINDS YOU OF "GREENWAY")
CARPET, CONVERSING ANIMATEDLY WITH OTHER DELEGATES.
THE FACT THAT YOUR TACITURN UNCLE HUGH IS THE
LAST PERSON YOU WOULD IMAGINE CHATTING AWAY TO
STRANGERS, IS IRRELEVANT — THE SHEER IMPROBABILITY
OF THE SCENE MAKES IT MORE MEMORABLE.

MEMORY AND SLEEP

Getting enough rest is vital if we wish to have a good memory – while we are asleep our brain consolidates the events of the day. Try a pre-sleep "breath meditation" to relax you into slumber. Close your eyes and take deep, slow breaths for 5 minutes. Try to make each complete breath last for a slow count of 10.

PRACTICE MAKES PERFECT

We have now covered five methods for memorizing names and faces. Although it is likely that you will find some easier than others, it is worth practising them all – some techniques work better than others in certain circumstances. And even the methods you find difficult at first will work well if you persevere and practise.

TOTAL RECALL

Here is a summary of what you have learned so far. When you meet someone new, asking yourself these questions will help you to decide which technique is likely to be the most useful in memorizing their name. Remember that your objective is to find a link between an instinctive association you make about the person and their name.

- Study their face and listen carefully to their name when you are introduced.

- Does their name remind you of a place?

- Does the person remind you of anyone familiar, such as a family member, a friend or a celebrity? ❯

- **What kind of trade or profession do you think the person might work in?**

- **Does the person have a particularly striking feature or appearance?**

- **Do you know anyone else who happens to have the same name?**

Always listen to your instinct when deciding which method of linking the name and the face is appropriate for the circumstances. And whichever technique you decide to use, build up as vivid and detailed a mental picture as you can – the more bizarre or surreal the image, the more memorable it will be.

MEMORY MEDITATION

To help you get the most out of memory techniques, before practising try this meditation to boost concentration. Close your eyes and slow your breathing. Visualize a white light floating just behind your eyes. Watch this light shrink as you breathe in and expand as you breathe out. Focus in this way for 5 minutes.

THE JOURNEY METHOD

You now know how to memorize individual people you meet. But what happens if you need to remember the names of a list of people who, say, will be attending an important meeting or a reception. This is not as difficult as it sounds because I have devised a tried-and-tested technique for remembering long lists – the Journey Method. ❯

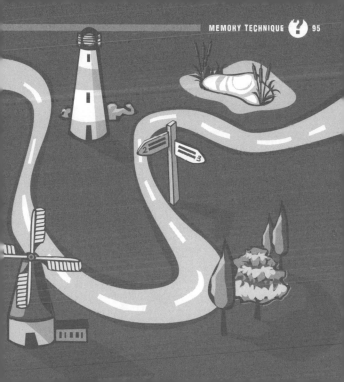

Here's how it works. Think of a journey that you know well, such as your daily walk to the station or the route you drive your children to school. Mentally recall the journey and as you do so, identify ten memorable fixed stages you pass along the way in the order that you come to them – for example the park, the corner shop, the flower stall, and so on. ›

Mentally walk through your journey several times to fix the stages in your mind. To memorize a list of people, place one name at each stage. Start by looking for a connection between the person's name and the particular stage of the journey. Then, link the name with the place as vividly as you can. ❯

LET'S LOOK AT A FEW EXAMPLES. SAY YOUR FIRST STAGE IS A POLICE STATION AND THE NAME YOU WISH TO PLACE THERE IS ROBERT WALKER. THE FIRST MENTAL PICTURE THAT COMES TO MY MIND IS OF A TALL, HOODED ROBBER HOLDING HIS BAG OF STOLEN GOODS AS HE WALKS UP THE STEPS INTO THE POLICE STATION, ACCOMPANIED BY TWO BURLY OFFICERS.

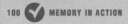

I MAKE THE IMAGE COME ALIVE BY IMAGINING AS MUCH DETAIL AS POSSIBLE. FOR EXAMPLE, I VISUALIZE THE CLOTHES THE ROBBER IS WEARING — JEANS AND A NAVY BLUE HOODED

SWEATSHIRT. IN MY MIND'S EYE I SEE ONE OF THE
POLICEMEN ANSWER A CALL ON HIS RADIO AS HE
APPROACHES THE ENTRANCE TO THE POLICE STATION;
AND I HEAR THE SIRENS OF POLICE CARS AS THEY
RETURN TO PARK UP IN THE STATION YARD. NOW TRY
TO THINK OF YOUR OWN IMAGE FOR ROBERT WALKER
AT THE POLICE STATION. ›

LET'S NOW MOVE ON TO THE SECOND STAGE ON YOUR JOURNEY, WHICH IS A PUBLIC TELEPHONE BOOTH. THE NAME OF THE PERSON IS MARION ARMSTRONG. THIS NAME IMMEDIATELY CONJURES UP IN MY MIND A VISION OF A BRIDE BECAUSE THE FIRST PART OF MARION SOUNDS LIKE "MARRY". MY BRIDE IS WEARING A TRADITIONAL LONG, WHITE DRESS AND A VEIL.

THEN I LINK IN THE SURNAME – ARMSTRONG – BY IMAGINING THE BRIDE STANDING IN THE PHONE BOOTH, EXERCISING HER VERY MUSCULAR, STRONG ARMS, USING THE PHONE RECEIVER AS A DUMBELL. UP AND DOWN, UP AND DOWN GOES HER RIGHT ARM, THEN SHE CHANGES OVER TO PUMP IRON WITH HER LEFT ARM.

YOU MIGHT FEEL THAT
THIS IMAGE IS RATHER
TONGUE-IN-CHEEK, BUT IT
IS PERFECTLY ACCEPTABLE TO
INTRODUCE AN ELEMENT OF HUMOUR, IF IT
HELPS MAKE YOUR ASSOCIATIONS MORE MEMORABLE.
NOW, IT'S YOUR TURN AGAIN TO THINK UP AS VIVID
AND DETAILED AN ASSOCIATION AS YOU CAN BETWEEN
MARION ARMSTRONG AND THE TELEPHONE BOOTH. >

It's time to put your newly aquired skills of using the journey method into practice. I would now like you to memorize the following list of ten celebrities in order, using your own ten-stage mental journey. Allow yourself 10 minutes.

1. Nicole Kidman
2. Bill Gates
3. Indira Gandhi
4. Charlie Chaplin
5. Greta Garbo
6. Al Gore
7. Venus Williams
8. Fred Astaire
9. Jennifer Lopez
10. Andy Warhol >

Now, WITHOUT LOOKING BACK AT THE NUMBERED LIST ON PAGE 104, REARRANGE THE LIST OF CELEBRITIES BELOW IN THE ORDER YOU MEMORIZED THEM. MENTALLY WALK YOUR JOURNEY RECALLING THE ASSOCIATIONS AND THE CELEBRITIES AS YOU DO SO.

FRED ASTAIRE
INDIRA GANDHI
ANDY WARHOL
NICOLE KIDMAN
CHARLIE CHAPLIN
JENNIFER LOPEZ
BILL GATES
VENUS WILLIAMS
AL GORE
GRETA GARBO

HOW DID YOU GET ON? WITH PRACTICE, YOU SHOULD
EASILY BE ABLE TO RECALL THE ORDER OF ALL TEN.

HERE'S ANOTHER LIST OF CELEBRITIES TO PRACTICE WITH:

1. JUDY GARLAND
2. RICHARD GERE
3. HILARY CLINTON
4. DENZEL WASHINGTON
5. DREW BARRYMORE
6. HENRY KISSINGER
7. CAMERON DIAZ
8. COLIN POWELL
9. OPRAH WINFREY
10. FRANK SINATRA

BUILD A STOCK OF JOURNEYS

Once you have mastered the Journey Method, you will be able to memorize long lists of people. As it is easier to remember several short journeys rather than one long journey, I suggest you start by thinking up several journeys of, say, ten stages each. You can then expand them to, say, 25 stages, when you get more confident.

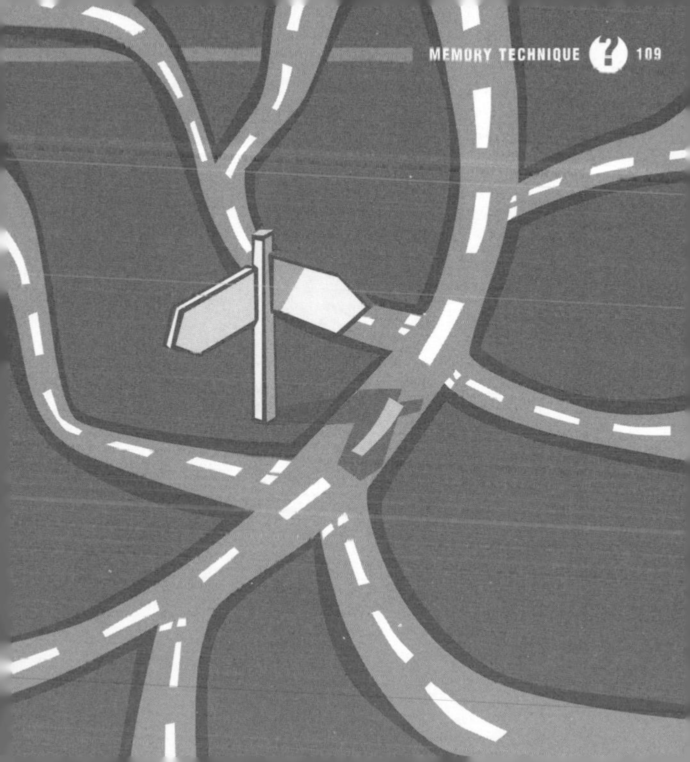

THE GOLDEN RULE OF MEMORY

Try to repeat and recall any memorizations you make at least five times to ensure that they are firmly embedded in your memory. For example, if you are using the Journey Method, mentally revisit each stage of your journey in the same order as you first made it, recreating fully each association as you go along.

EXPAND THE PICTURE

As you become more proficient at linking names to faces, you can memorize more information about someone you meet by introducing extra elements into the mental picture. For example, if we return to Robert Walker (see pp.100–101), you could memorize the fact that his hobby is fishing, by imagining his swag bag being full of pungent fish! ❯

LET'S LOOK AT SOME MORE EXAMPLES. EARLIER (SEE P.74) WE MET ANGELA MARSHALL WHOSE MOST STRIKING FEATURE WAS HER WING-SHAPED GLASSES. YOU MAY NOW WISH TO NOTE THAT SHE RUNS HER OWN KNITWEAR BUSINESS AND THAT SHE IS A TEETOTALER. TO ADD IN THESE EXTRA PIECES OF INFORMATION, YOU IMAGINE ANGELA SITTING IN HER COTTAGE, KNITTING (HER KNITWEAR BUSINESS IS A COTTAGE INDUSTRY), A CUP OF HOT TEA STEAMING ON THE TABLE IN FRONT OF HER.

OR, TAKE YOUR NEW AQUAINTANCE CIARAN O'GRADY, WHO YOU THOUGHT LOOKED LIKE A CHEF (SEE P.66). SAY YOU NOW NEED TO REMEMBER THAT HE HAS AN IDENTICAL TWIN AND THAT HE SPEAKS FRENCH. YOU IMAGINE CIARAN UNLOCKING THE KITCHEN DOOR AND MAKING GRAVY AS BEFORE, BUT THIS TIME ACCOMPANIED BY A SECOND, IDENTICAL CIARAN WHO IS PREPARING FRENCH BEANS.

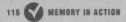

IN THE WORLD MEMORY CHAMPIONSHIPS, THERE IS AN EVENT CALLED "NAMES AND FACES" IN WHICH THE CONTESTANTS HAVE TO COMMIT TO MEMORY, AND THEN RECALL, AS MANY NAMES THAT GO WITH SPECIFIC FACES AS POSSIBLE.

IF YOU WOULD LIKE TO SEE WHETHER YOU HAVE WORLD-CLASS POTENTIAL IN THIS EVENT, TRY THE FOLLOWING TEST, WHICH IS BASED ON THE WORLD MEMORY CHAMPIONSHIPS EVENT.

GATHER TOGETHER PHOTOGRAPHS OF 99 PEOPLE FROM MAGAZINES AND NEWSPAPERS AND CUT THEM OUT.

WRITE EACH PERSON'S FORE- AND SURNAME ON THE BACK OF THEIR PHOTOGRAPH. (DON'T CHOOSE FAMOUS PEOPLE WHOSE NAMES YOU ALREADY KNOW — THAT WOULD GIVE YOU AN UNFAIR ADVANTAGE!)

SPEND **15** MINUTES MEMORIZING THE FACES AND THEIR CORRESPONDING NAMES, TAKING GOOD NOTE OF HOW THE NAMES ARE SPELLED. THEN, SHUFFLE THE >

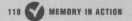

PHOTOGRAPHS AND, LOOKING AGAIN AT EACH IN TURN, TRY TO RECALL THE FULL NAME THAT GOES WITH THE FACE. WRITE DOWN YOUR ANSWERS. (EVEN IF YOU CAN ONLY REMEMBER THE FIRST NAME OR THE SURNAME, WRITE IT DOWN AS IT WILL STILL COUNT.)

WHEN YOU HAVE FINISHED, CHECK YOUR WRITTEN ANSWERS AGAINST THE NAMES YOU WROTE ON THE BACK OF THE PHOTOGRAPHS. AWARD YOURSELF 2 POINTS IF YOU GOT THE WHOLE NAME RIGHT, AND 1 POINT IF YOU RECALLED ONE PART OF THE NAME CORRECTLY. YOU MUST ALSO DEDUCT HALF A POINT FOR EVERY SPELLING ERROR.

HOW DID YOU DO? IF YOU HAD A SCORE OF 50+ (WITH 25 OR MORE CORRECT FULL NAMES), YOU HAVE CHAMPIONSHIP POTENTIAL, SO KEEP PRACTISING. MAYBE WE'LL MEET AT THE NEXT WORLD MEMORY CHAMPIONSHIPS!